Walking with Grace

Walking with Grace

Lessons in Courage, Passion,
and Defying Gravity

By Grace Killelea

For my mom, Audemia Ozvalda Killelea

*She made me believe it was
possible to defy gravity.*

INTRODUCTION

There are moments in life when you can stay in the heartbreak or you can create a breakthrough. Moments when you move from pissed off to passionate. Moments when the universe shifts because one more wonderful soul has left the earth. Moments when you know that somewhere deep in your core there is something you can do to make a difference. Moments when you move beyond what holds you down, moments when you defy gravity. On Friday, March 26, 2009, I had one of those moments.

As the facilitator of a wonderful executive leadership program for women, I am often asked to share news that affects our community of amazing women leaders. On this day, I received a call asking me to share the news that one of our own, Mary White, had died. Mary was a strong, capable leader who blazed the trail for women executives in the cable industry. Mary was often honored by her colleagues and was even named a Wonder Woman, one of the most prestigious awards a female executive can receive in the cable industry. She was one of the few female presidents in a male-dominated field. She was a mentor, teacher, guide, coach, daughter, wife, mother, and soul sister. She was a wonder woman all around.

I only knew Mary peripherally, but there was something about her dying that really shook me. In a world with only six degrees of separation, there was only one degree of separation between Mary and me. I had laughed and kibitzed with her friends. I applauded her awards and accolades in the industry. She represented all of the women that I interact with, and even though she wasn't *my* dear friend, she was *a* dear friend to women I know and love. I thought about all of the worlds that were going to be touched by her death. All of these universes would be grieving because this one person was gone.

I remember getting the call in my office and just crying my eyes out. It was a deep, overwhelming sadness that would not lift. I left work and went to meet with a friend, and I cried all through lunch. When I went home, I cried some more. The day Mary died, she was in her late forties and the mother of a teenage girl. I was a fifty-year-old woman with no children, and I weighed over three hundred pounds.

That next morning my tears were spent, and I was angry. I was angry that so many women have to live in a world where breast cancer becomes their reality. The number of women in my own life—friends, coworkers, and sisters in spirit—with breast cancer just seemed to multiply every day. Somehow, in all of that anger, I started to consider my own life. I was morbidly obese, and the clock was ticking for me. I suddenly felt as if daylight was burning and I was running out of chances to save my own life. I remember thinking that if Mary White had the option to get off the couch and take a walk instead of losing her eyesight and suffering through repeated rounds of chemo, which would she have chosen? What would she have done to have another day with her daughter? And then I asked myself, what was I willing to do to save my own life?

That moment was a perfect storm of fear, sadness, and anger. I graduated from pissed off to passionate. So, I signed up for The Walk, a sixty-mile walk completed over three days. Before I could change my mind, I sent an e-mail out to over five hundred people announcing my intentions to walk and to prove that I was making a physical commitment—not just a financial one—to help end breast cancer. I didn't talk the idea over with anyone first. I just sat down in my big, comfy chair, signed up, and then sent the e-mail to my network. And just like that, all of that passion turned to panic and fear. I had committed myself in a very public way to something that I didn't honestly believe I could achieve. I had never done anything that physically demanding in my life. It wasn't long before I started to anticipate my future humiliation.

Walking with Grace is my story of moving through all of the moments of this journey, of how I decided to move beyond my fear one moment at a time. It is my story of how I started on the road of physical and spiritual healing in a sweaty, inglorious, and ungraceful way. I started a blog to track my journey and called it Fat Girl Walking. This book is a summary of that blog: a day-by-day account of my major triumphs and minor mishaps as I did my best to walk with grace. Sprinkled throughout these pages are my tributes to some of the most courageous women I know—women who are defying gravity every day in their fight against this horrific disease. These are women who have all gone to war with the cancer dragon and won.

I hope this book will serve to inspire someone else to get off the couch and do something extraordinary in his or her lifetime—to defy gravity.

Whatever your passion, I hope my story gives you the inspiration to take that first step with grace and gratitude. I know that if I can defy gravity, then you can, too!

CONTENTS

Fundraising Flash #1

March 2009

Dear Friends and Supporters,

This week another fantastic woman I know died of breast cancer. In the past ninety days, five women I know personally have either been diagnosed with, had surgery for, or had a recurrence of the disease. I am angry. I am angry that these women have to live in a world where they have to slay this dragon. Although I am blessed with good health, I am overweight and out of shape. I have decided to channel my anger and energy into doing something proactive.

I have taken on an incredible personal challenge. On October 16 through 18, I'll be walking sixty miles over the course of three days, camping out at night with thousands of other women and men taking this journey with me. Today, I am still one hundred pounds overweight. I am terrified by this physical challenge but those of you who know me know I believe in breaking free of the things that hold you down. This is my way to defy gravity.

Without a cure, one in eight women in the United States will continue to be diagnosed with breast cancer. I plan on shattering my goal of raising five thousand dollars to help bring us closer to the cure. That's why I'm walking The Walk: because everyone deserves a lifetime.

I would like to shatter my fundraising goal by July 4, Independence Day, so don't delay!

I appreciate your support, and if you are willing, I ask you to spread the word to your network of friends and colleagues who might want to participate as well!

I am planning on forming Team Defy Gravity for The Walk. If you are interested in joining me, please drop me a note.

Grace

CHAPTER 1

FAT GIRL WALKING

Sixty miles is overwhelming, but you know how you walk sixty miles? You walk one step at a time. That's really it ... and it doesn't have to be graceful or pretty ... you just have to move.

—Grace

Day 1: Scared out of My Mind

Okay, I've taken the plunge. I am signed up. I'm committing myself to The Walk, and I am hoping to form a team. I am more than one hundred pounds overweight, and I have a long way to go to be fit enough to walk sixty miles in three days. But I am mad, and when I get mad, I take action. I downloaded my training roster today and am getting lots of advice from my friends who are runners. Apparently, socks are a big deal. Who knew? So, here's to all the broads in my life who have been touched by breast cancer, and here's to all the fifty somethings who feel they need to take better control of their lives. This fat girl walked forty minutes today. It's a start.

Day 2: Unbelievable

I am so honored and blessed. I had hoped to raise five thousand dollars by July 4, and thanks to the generosity of my friends, this goal was achieved in twenty-four hours!

So, I did my two miles tonight at the gym at work. I admit, it's a little tough to walk in and see so many fit people in one place, but I did it anyway and walked my two miles on the treadmill. I am very excited that my first teammate signed up today. Sherita is the first official team member of Team Defy Gravity, and I am thrilled that she is joining me on this journey. Two miles tomorrow!

Day 7: A Choice

I am in a hotel room in Chicago, and tomorrow morning, I will be heading to Madison, Wisconsin for Mary White's funeral. Mary was only forty-seven years old when she died of breast cancer. Today, I choose to do what I can to take care of my own health and to help in the fight against this terrible disease. Tomorrow, we will celebrate the life of a great woman. I choose to honor her and all of the other wonder women I know who have been touched by cancer. I will do a slow three miles in the morning before we head to Madison.

Day 10: One Step at a Time

Yesterday was Mary White's funeral. She was a remarkable woman, and the love of her friends and family was so evident. Breast cancer never defeated her, but it did take her much too soon. I am reminding myself that the goal of fighting this disease is equal to my goal of fighting my own issues with my health and weight. I have to take this one step at a time and keep moving even when I am tired and feeling overwhelmed.

She Defies Gravity

ELAINE

In our circle of friends, Elaine is known as the "Texas Tornado." She is a warrior woman. Elaine is fit, smart, strong, and capable. Elaine and I were in Las Vegas together for a conference and I remember being so happy to be having dinner with this amazing woman in one of my favorite cities.

Elaine was facilitating a session for a group of women leaders I work with, and it was a treat to have one-on-one time with her at dinner. I noticed she had been sitting down through much of her session, but she blamed it on a leg injury, and I didn't question it.

Our dinner started with the usual chitchat and catch-up. Elaine's husband had a stroke a year or so before, and they were still finding their way in their new world. Somewhere between the breadbasket and our fish course, Elaine looked me in the eye and said, "I have breast cancer, and the reason I've been sitting down is because I just finished a round of chemo and I'm exhausted." So, here, in my favorite city, in a fabulous hotel with lovely food, my beautiful friend who I think of as my own personal "wise woman" told me she had cancer.

All I wanted to do in that moment was hug Elaine and take care of her. She told me how awful the chemo was and that she was exhausted and uncomfortable all the time. I asked her if I could arrange for her to go for a long massage at the hotel. (Now, I know massages don't cure cancer, but they sure as heck can heal the soul.) So, with her cute, stylish wig, she smiled and said she would love a massage.

The day after Elaine told me her news, she and I were together in a conference session where a man in our group started describing how the key to negotiation for women is to use our sex. He suggested that we should "cry if we have to" and maybe even "show a little cleavage now and again." Elaine had a tough morning with the side effects of her chemo, and her energy level was very low. As this jerk kept talking, I felt my blood pressure rising. Elaine leaned over to me with her sweet Texas drawl in its full glory and said just above a whisper, "You know he has to die right?" I literally snorted my drink out of my nose, I laughed so hard.

Elaine had breast cancer, but breast cancer didn't steal her spirit or her sense of humor. She kept moving forward, step by step and day by day. Somewhere along the way, during her journey to slay the cancer dragon, I started calling her "Lil' Bit" because, despite her huge spirit, she's actually a very petite person. At the end of The Walk, one of my dearest memories was leading our group into the closing ceremonies with Lil' Bit by my side. Today, Elaine is cancer free and whirling through life because that's what tornados do!

CHAPTER 2

GRATITUDE

I think when you are faced with something as devastating as a cancer diagnosis, that somewhere in your day you must still find a source of gratitude. Even if it is a nanosecond of laughing at yourself or appreciating something that someone has done, that is what lifts you out of that dark place. You have to ask yourself, "Do you want to pull the dirt up over your head or do you want to dig your way out? Do you want to find the light or do you want to turn the light off?" Gratitude is a source of light.

—Grace

Day 20: Checking under the Hood

I'm on the train to New York City to see my doctor. Nothing serious, but I need to go fix some things so I can travel next week. I didn't walk yesterday as planned. I overslept and then didn't return from New York until midnight. This morning, my 6:00 walk turned into a 6:00 hurry-up-and-get-dressed-to-catch-the-train-to-New York. I am completely without a voice (stop cheering, out there!) due to acid reflux-induced laryngitis. Oy! So, that is what I need to take care of today. This afternoon, I have a mammogram, and in between, I am working and walking! I am blessed to have medical coverage and the flexibility to go take care of myself.

Day 23: Filled with Gratitude

I am in San Diego on business and walked my three miles this morning. A couple of nice things happened along the way.

I was able to talk and walk while I was walking a 3.5-mile-per-hour pace at the end of my walk. I have been able to walk up and down a very large flight of stairs here at the hotel without being winded. I am down a size since January. I am filled with gratitude today.

Day 26: Go Team!

I am so excited to have had three teammates sign up so far! I walked 1.5 miles yesterday but started to develop a couple of heel blisters, so I erred on the side of caution and stopped. I took today off, but I am walking tomorrow morning before my workday starts. I am having dinner tomorrow night with three high school girlfriends. One of those friends, Marianne, has just started chemo. She was one of my dearest friends from that time in my life, and I can't wait to see her again. I hate that she has to go through this. Tomorrow morning, it's Marianne's gorgeous face that's going to get this fat girl walking.

Day 29: Finding My Inner Athlete

I walked for two hours today. It was a little hard (my feet started cramping), but I did it without quitting or getting blisters. Wow! I am feeling stronger and told myself that I walked one-fourth of one day of the three-day walk because a day of walking is typically eight hours. It's important that I consider training as an important part of my day and my lifestyle. No going back now. I am going to find my inner athlete and let her start to be in charge!

Day 32: Shout out to Suzy

I walked forty-five minutes today in the middle of Washington DC with my wonderful friend, Susan Patten. We were up at 5:30 AM and walked and talked. It was great. So many of my gal pals are offering to walk with me to keep me motivated and strong!

By the way, my friend Suzy is starting her chemo today. I'm sending her love and enough good mojo to kick that cancer's butt!

Tomorrow is my day off from walking, but I'm going to do some work for my team. I love the fantastic women who are signing up to join me on this journey and could not imagine walking without them.

She Defies Gravity

SUZY

Suzy is a leader at the same company I work for but is based in Connecticut. We have worked together remotely on and off for years. Because I'm really twelve years old at heart, somewhere along the line I started calling Suzy "Tutti Fruity." Right around the time Mary White died, I heard the news that Suzy had been diagnosed with breast cancer, too, and that she would be having surgery very soon.

For awhile, it felt like every day after Mary passed that I was hearing about another woman being diagnosed. At that time in my life, I knew more than eight women who had died from, were diagnosed with, were in the middle of chemo for, or were in some stage of their treatment for breast cancer. When I heard about Suzy, I reached out to her right away via telephone. Then, I wrote her an e-mail very soon after our first chat and begged her to "kick her cancer's butt."

And she did. When Suzy heard about The Walk, she wrote to me and told me how much she wanted to join Team Defy Gravity (TDG). Unfortunately, she would be going through chemotherapy while we were training, but it was the easiest decision in the world to make Suzy a member of our team. We knew she was in the fight of her life, and we knew that she would not be able to physically walk with us. But Suzy said she wanted to walk the last mile with the team, and I knew we were going to make that happen.

Suzy lost her hair, and the chemo was tough, but every time I spoke to her, she was upbeat and so excited about being part of TDG. She was part of our e-mail chains and got people to raise money for our team. She had such a great attitude. On the weekend of the walk, Suzy and her husband came down to Philly and joined us along the route.

One of my greatest memories of that day was finding Suzy in the crowd and having her and Elaine (Lil' Bit) on either arm as we led the walk into the closing ceremony. Imagine two itty-bitty blonde women, both cancer survivors, and this big, redheaded woman in the middle. We were quite the sight.

In 2010 Suzy helped form Team Defy Gravity II and completed The Walk in Boston. "Go, Tutti Fruity, go!"

CHAPTER 3

CALLING OUT MY CRAZY

*I was really afraid that I couldn't physically do it.
I thought I might be too overweight to walk. I thought it
was over for me. I worried I would be the fattest person at
the race. I have a lot of years of being made fun of and
often wondered, "Can I really freaking do this?"*

—Grace

DAY 33: Straight to Crazy

Today was a day off from training, but I am scheduled to do four miles tomorrow. Looks like I will be doing my walk-at-home video tapes because it is supposed to rain most of the day. I am walking, but my eating is crappy. I am eating too much and really need to make some better choices. I know that when I am stressed and tired my tendency is to comfort myself with food. I won't make excuses here. I'm just calling out my crazy because if you are crazy, you should at least acknowledge it and give it a name.

DAY 35: Working It Out

I have a very busy week ahead, and then I'm flying to Seattle on Thursday. I'm still overeating, but I'm packing my walking gear!

DAY 38: Pushing through It

I made myself do two miles this morning. I am having pretty bad tooth pain, and I have a second visit to an endodontist scheduled. I am working from home for the rest of the day. I made myself walk when I got up because I knew I would blow it off today. I really, really didn't want to work out today, so I compromised and told myself I only had to walk two miles. So, now it's done, and I don't have to think about it anymore today.

DAY 43: Praying for Strength

I walked three miles this morning. I think my walking is going pretty well, and the fundraising is really off to a terrific start, but my eating is still awful. If it's not nailed down, I am eating it. I am telling the truth about my food because it would be so easy to lie. Of course, when you are one hundred pounds overweight, folks tend to do the math themselves. I hate this.

In slaying the cancer dragon news: I heard from my friend Suzy. She shaved her head and donated her hair to Locks of Love. My friend Marianne wrote and is toughing it out with her second round of chemo. I love these women and am so amazed at their strength and grace during this challenging time. I pray I find my own strength to take better care of myself. What is it that keeps me stuck in the crazy?

DAY 46: Just What I Needed

So, I was really grousing about not wanting to do my workout tape and just told myself to shut up and do it. I popped in a five-mile workout tape I haven't done before and couldn't stop laughing. One of the women in the tape looks just like me! She has red hair and is about my shape and size. We look enough alike that if any of my pals saw it, they would think it was me. So, even though I wanted to quit around three miles, I figured, "Hey, if she can do it, I can do it," and I finished all five miles. It was just the motivation I needed today.

Fundraising Flash #2

June 2009

Hello Friends and Colleagues,

Many of you know I have committed to walk in The Walk to raise money and awareness to find the cure for breast cancer. In the last twelve months, too many women in my life have either been diagnosed with or lost their battle to this disease. Every woman diagnosed with breast cancer is one woman too many! I am channeling my anger into something positive, and I committed to walk sixty miles in three days as a symbol of support. I had originally planned to raise five thousand dollars, and thanks to the unbelievable generosity of my network, today I have raised over twenty-three thousand dollars. My goal is to reach thirty thousand dollars.

The money goes directly to funding breast cancer research, and I am thrilled to tell you I have ten fantastic women who have agreed to join me in this journey. We have named ourselves Team Defy Gravity, and as a team, we plan on shattering a goal of fifty thousand dollars. Some of you have asked about the name Team Defy Gravity, so I thought I'd explain. Taken from one of my favorite songs from the Broadway musical *Wicked,* gravity is anything invisible that holds you down. For too long, I have allowed my fear of doing anything physical and of exercise keep me from doing something like this. So, the team name is a reminder to me to move beyond that which holds me down.

Together, Team Defy Gravity will walk October 16–18 in Philadelphia, and we will be walking for the friends, sisters, daughters, coworkers, wives, and grandmothers who have been fighting this disease. Personally, I am using this walk as a way to tackle my own demons and to take control of my own health challenges. I have started a blog called Fat Girl Walking to chronicle my journey.

Any and all support of this cause is appreciated. I am unbelievably blessed to have people like you in my life. For those of you who have already made a donation, thank you from the bottom of my heart.

I hope you defy gravity today!

Grace

CHAPTER 4

TIRED AND UNINSPIRED

Were there days that I didn't train? Absolutely!
Were there days that I sat and ate ice cream? Yup!

—Grace

DAY 48: You Want Some Cheese with that Whine?

Okay, so I've got a crazy travel schedule this week. Florida today and Los Angeles at the end of the week, which means I have to be very mindful of getting my walking in. So far, not so good. I didn't pack my shoes or gear because I had a 6:00 AM flight, which means I won't walk today. I should have brought my stuff.

I will walk tomorrow after work because I have no choice. It's so easy to get caught up in how tired I am and to feel badly for poor me. So, I checked in with Suzy. She is having an icky time with her chemo. Hmmm, let's think about this. Suzy is dealing with chemo. Grace just doesn't want to move her butt. Yep, the results are in. I have no reason to complain. So, I'm logging five miles tomorrow come hell or high water. Chemo sucks, but walking is just no big damn deal.

DAY 49: New Day

Wow, I'm tired. I got up at 3:45 this morning so I could get on a 6:00 flight back to Philly. I ended up having a medical procedure this afternoon that was pretty uncomfortable, so I didn't lace up my shoes today. Now, I'm packing for my twenty-four-hour turnaround to Los Angeles. I am blessed beyond belief to have these kinds of problems to complain about.

I am, however, committed to telling the truth about my walking and health here. I have a couple of medical issues to explore, none of which are helped by being out of shape. Walking is not just about raising money for the cure; it's about improving the quality of my life.

DAY 50: OMG!

Picture yourself walking on the treadmill in the gym at your hotel after a large Mexican meal full of beans. That was me. I had to cut the walk short because I was mortified someone would come in and I would be responsible for making their eyes water. I walked two miles in perfect solitude and decided to quit while I was ahead. I walked out sweaty and wishing I could have sprayed the place with air freshener when Mr. I–live-in-LA-have-six-pack-abs-only-use-designer-hair-gel-didn't-you-see-the-TV-pilot-I-was-in walked through the door. My guess? He decided to go running outside instead! Yes, I really was mortified.

DAY 55: Packed the Shoes

Just arrived in St. Paul, where I am working for the next few days. I am committed to doing an hour on the treadmill in the morning. I packed my gear, so I have no excuses. I have a very hectic schedule while I am here, so the best time for me to get my walking in is in the early morning. I had to say no to someone today, and that's hard for me. I was asked to sit on a board for a group I really like, but I just can't do it justice. One thing I am trying to strive for is self-care because it's not my strong suit. However, I'm proud that I said no to adding more to my already-packed schedule. It's a first step. And I walked three miles this morning!

Day 57: Igloos on My Feet

So, I looked down while I was walking today and had to laugh out loud. My feet are huge in my new walking shoes. From the top, each foot has this big white dome that makes them look like igloos. I had my feet measured, and they are now size 10 1/2 EE. Them's some feet! So, as I've aged, my feet have gotten wider and longer? Well, they aren't pretty, but they do get me from place to place, and I can still dance when I hear a song I love. And I walked just short of three miles today.

Day 58: We ain't last!

Sherita and I attended the official Walk kickoff in Cherry Hill, New Jersey, yesterday. We did a three-mile training walk, and the good news is we weren't last! We walked in the rain (I was going to tell you it was a tsunami, but Sherita insisted I tell the truth), and we were both really pleased to have finished in the middle of the group. We know it's not a race, and we both could have used a bit more stretching before we started, but it was really great not to be the last two gals over the finish line. The walk was only three miles, but there were security folks making sure we were safe and knew the route. It was pretty cool.

We walked by some folks holding signs, and I, of course, was convinced they were there as a cheering section. As it turns out, there was a car wash happening. (I really am an egomaniac.) But at the end of the walk, there were some folks holding up signs for us, so that was nice. Sherita and I had our picture taken to commemorate our walk. We had a great time!

Fundraising Flash #3

July 2009

My Dear Friends and Colleagues,

I am humbled and grateful to have been the recipient of your kindness and generosity. As of last Wednesday, with your help and donations, I was able to raise thirty thousand dollars for the Breast Cancer Walk. As you know, my journey started with a note written when the fantastic Mary White passed away. My goal that day was to raise five thousand dollars by July 4. Well, you answered the call, and I received five thousand dollars in less than twenty-four hours of sending that first e-mail.

I have known for a very long time that I have been blessed with a network of smart, kind, generous, funny, and supportive people. What I didn't know was how deep you would dig and how much you would invest in reading my blog and cheering me on as I face the challenge of walking sixty miles. I am still scared of this very physical challenge and am training to get myself into shape. Even if I don't lose a pound, I am stronger and have more stamina than when I started a couple of months ago. In my fiftieth year, it is a miracle for me to be facing my version of a marathon.

Here is just a glimpse of what keeps me motivated. Last Wednesday, I was $640 short of my $30,000 goal. While on the treadmill doing my training, I received a notification that a $640 donation had been made to my walk. I soon discovered that the donor was a dear, old friend I had lost touch with, a friend I was with when she was told she had breast cancer. I remember how frightened and brave she was, and I remember praying to God every night that she would be okay. I remember watching her hair fall out and thinking how unfair it was that she had to fight such a fight.

Many years later, she is cancer free and has done the three-day walk herself many times. She was the first woman

I ever knew who was diagnosed with this nasty disease. I am sorry to say she was not the last, but her donation put me to the top. Thank you, Judy. I will always love you for this sweet gesture.

Wherever you are when you read this note, whatever kind of day you are having, whatever stress you have been carrying today, please put it down for a moment and know that you helped me defy gravity.

Sending you an ocean of gratitude,

Grace

She Defies Gravity

JUDY

The nurse told me that if anything bad was going on, she would come and get me out of the waiting room. A few minutes later, she opened the door, and that's how I found out my best friend Judy had breast cancer.

It was the nineties. We were single, working on our careers, always on a diet and talking about men and relationships. Suddenly this wonderful woman in my life who had found a lump but had tried to convince me it was nothing was sitting in a room fifteen feet away and feeling her world crumble apart. When I walked into the room, Judy was as pale as a ghost, and she looked up with tears in her eyes and said the words, "I have cancer." After heading out of the doctor's office, we did what any self respecting gal pals do after hearing such devastating news: we went to lunch.

During lunch, someone put the song "Crazy" by Patsy Cline on the jukebox, and my brave and beautiful friend burst into tears because that was her mom's favorite song, and her mom had recently passed away. So, here we are eating, Judy is sobbing and telling me she doesn't want to die, and people are staring. All I could think of to get her to stop crying was to tell her that everyone probably thought we were a couple, and I was breaking up with her. It was just one of those moments, but it worked.

Judy pushed through chemo and radiation. I watched her hair fall out and tried to make her laugh by trying on the silliest wigs when we went shopping for hair. I applauded her when she decided to rock her bald look everywhere she went, claiming wigs were just too hot. She was surrounded by family and friends, and I was just one of the many folks who went on the journey with her. Judy stared her cancer in the eye and spit at it. She was not going to roll over. She was the first woman

I ever knew who did The Walk, and she has gone out to walk many times since. Judy has been in remission for years now, and she is an advocate for women who are still at war with this insidious disease.

For all the stupid reasons friends lose touch, Judy and I left each other's lives in the late nineties and didn't speak or connect for years. But then she found me on Facebook in 2009 after I had committed to do The Walk. Judy asked if we could connect, and of course I agreed. So, one night we spoke on the phone, and the years just fell away. Today, Judy is a constant light in my life, and I'm grateful that she continues to defy gravity.

CHAPTER 5

CAN'T STOP, WON'T STOP

I have something called a "hell no" button, and I have known about it for years. Sometimes, I wish I had pushed it sooner, but there is something in me that will absolutely not allow me to be defeated by my circumstances. I get to a point where I literally say, "Hell no! This is not the life I'm meant to live."

—Grace

DAY 60: Vegas, Baby

I'm celebrating my fiftieth birthday this Saturday with about 120 pals, and I am very excited. The weather here in Vegas is hot but gorgeous, and I am so thrilled. Here's to being a strong, fit woman for the second half of this amazing life I have!

DAY 65: Really?

It has been a mad rush lately. My birthday celebration was fantabulous! I kept my training up while in Vegas and left a business dinner early on Tuesday night so I could get to the gym. I have had business dinners every night this week, so it's been tough. There have been lots of times when I tell myself I don't have to walk, and then I just say, "Really?" Because sixty miles is a long way to walk if you're out of shape and haven't trained. That keeps me going.

DAY 71: Weekend Update

I sent another fundraising e-mail out this weekend. I have been trying to push to my goal of thirty thousand dollars, and I have less than six thousand dollars to go. I am very excited. Team Defy Gravity is really starting to gel, and everyone is rallying around both finding sponsors and walking. My eating is still crappy, so I haven't lost a single pound.

DAY 72: Oh, Happy Day!

Great news! Yesterday, my two friends Suzy and Marianne both finished their chemo. I know this has been a tough time for the two of them, and they have both been so positive and forward-focused through all of their treatments. Everyone I know has a woman in their life that has been touched by breast cancer, and every one is one woman too many. I am walking after work today. I am going to do four to five miles. Chemo sucks, but walking is just not that big of a deal.

DAY 73: Big Girl MRI

I walked an hour last night with Deb. It was a crazy day. I had to have an MRI, and I have never had one before. Well, if you haven't had an MRI, let me paint the picture. Imagine being the inside part of a sausage. Imagine being shoved into a tube, and while you are in the tube, lots of jackhammers are banging on the outside of it. And if that's not delightful enough, I'm a big woman. I am a size 20 or 22. I was wedged into this thing so tightly the blood flow to my arms was being cut off.

So, now I'm shoved into the tube. The jackhammers are going, and I am thinking if it was so damn hard to get me in here, how do they get me out? I actually started to feel anxious, which is really unusual for me. I know I sound like a big baby in light of what my friends have been going through, but it was pretty awful.

Now, here's the kicker. They finally pull me out, my heart is in my throat, and with embarrassment and disbelief, I say to the medical technician, "I know I'm a big woman, but I am certainly not the biggest person you have had in here. How do you fit folks like that into the machine?" And she says, "Oh we have a bigger machine. We just didn't schedule you over there because we figured we could squeeze you into this one." Can you believe it?

Lesson learned. Just as I know not to shop in the regular-sized clothing section of the mall—I shop at Lane Bryant's—I now know to ask for the plus-sized MRI machine.

Although my goal someday soon is *not* to need to pay attention to this kind of thing, it was still embarrassing, scary, uncomfortable, anxiety-inducing, and totally unnecessary. I cried the entire way home.

DAY 81: Seven Miles!

I have been swamped at work and haven't had the time to do my updates. But I have been keeping up my training, and this morning, Sherita and I walked 7.4 miles, which is my longest walk so far. I feel awesome! I now know I could do 10 miles, and I'm going to do it next weekend. I am also going to start adding inclines on the treadmill to really kick it into gear. Sherita and I had a great time just walking and talking and getting to know each other. She has been a blessing, and she is so darn funny! It was Big Girls Walking today. We must be quite the sight walking on the path. People really do just get out of our way.

Work is kicking my butt, but I'm committed to keeping my training up. By the way, Team Defy Gravity is still growing; we need less than $5,000 and we will reach our $30,000 goal.

DAY 84: Expired Warranty?

I didn't walk this weekend, but I am committing to a three-mile walk in the morning before I go to work. I have a busy week ahead, and I am making my walking a priority. I am seeing a doctor in Philly on Wednesday about my lap band. Keep your fingers crossed. I could use some help getting my food intake aligned with all of this exercise. I am eating everything that's not nailed down. My health has to be a priority. It looks like something funky with my hip showed up on my MRI, so I have yet another thing to go get checked out. Did my warranty expire?

DAY 88: Not Going to Stop

There is a lot of activity in my life right now. Maybe too much. I had to literally squeeze my walk in tonight, but I did 2.8 miles on the treadmill and will get the rest done in my walk home. I am three levels below exhausted, but I know I can't stop. Everything will snowball into not walking at all, and I'll lose the momentum I have right now. But honestly, I am beat. I am going to try and stick to high-protein foods to help manage my weight. When I'm stressed, I eat, and I don't want to gain twenty or thirty extra pounds now.

CHAPTER 6

WALKING THE WALK

This was an overwhelming commitment of time, but
I have the blessing of being the queen of my own world.
I am in awe of people with families who add this to their lives.

—Grace

DAY 92: Strategic Walking

We are sixteen weeks away from The Walk, and I am feeling the days speed by. My schedule has intensified to a really large degree. With that said, I need to consider my walking time as part of my life strategy. It's time to think and clear my head. I have to block out my walking time a week in advance. It's the only way I will get my training done. I took this weekend off, though. I slept in (my body was really sleep-deprived) and just let myself move at a natural pace.

This has been an interesting week. Michael Jackson died, and he was only fifty years old, just a few months older than me. And today, Billie Mays—who was also just fifty—died. It just reminds me that nothing is guaranteed. Life is just so fleeting. I don't want to be about gloom and doom, but this wave of death has been very sobering indeed.

DAY 94: Training

I walked two miles yesterday, which is all the time I had. I worked until 9:00 PM, so it was a long day. Today, I have my gear with me, and my pal Barb and I are walking after work. We plan to walk a solid hour. Barb is a tiny little thing, but man, she walks fast! I hope I can keep up with her. Here's a big shout out to my gal pals who are fighting their fight today. I love you!

DAY 96: Yes, I Can!

I *can* walk and *will* walk sixty miles, strong, healthy, without injury. Yes, I can!

DAY 100: Still Fat Girl Walking

So we are fourteen weeks away from the walk. I haven't lost a single pound! I am pretty darn sure that has a lot to do with my terrible eating habits, but I am still training, still walking. I did between five and six miles last night and am going to do five miles on the treadmill tonight before I go home. I am pretty frustrated with my eating and myself. My lap band is wide open (long story), and my head and my stomach haven't been in sync since I was five years old. I will walk, though, but let's just hope I improve my health in the meantime.

DAY 107: Me Tired

Back home from work at 10:00 PM. It was a long, long day, and I honestly don't have the energy to walk tonight. I promised myself when I started this journey that I would be honest. So, here it is. My walking mojo is a little fuzzy right now. I'm tired and overwhelmed, and I am having a tough time getting enough sleep. Tomorrow, I will do three miles at the gym after work, and Deb promised to walk eleven miles with me on Saturday, but yikes, me tired.

Day 109: I Found My Boom! Boom! Pow!

I just did five miles on the treadmill! I feel my mojo. I'm digging deep. I know it's there. Thank you for loving me despite the valleys.

DAY 111: Broke Ten Miles!

I walked eleven miles today! I admit I was a little queasy when I stopped walking, but I feel better now. I was talking to a friend who reminded me that even if I haven't lost a pound, which I haven't, the fact that I can walk eleven miles straight is a victory. I am building up my stamina. For a woman who has *never* exercised in her entire life, this is pretty cool. I am not thrilled when I walk, but I am feeling pretty proud of myself today. I'm sending out good mojo to all the women in my life I love.

DAY 118: Big Girls Walking Twelve Miles

We survived our longest walk ever, twelve miles! Sherita and I started at 6:00 AM and walked for just over four hours. I am really proud of us. Neither one of us has ever been athletic, so this was a big personal accomplishment for us both. We will be up bright and early again tomorrow morning to walk six miles. I am really, really proud of us "big girls." I am also really, really glad to be home in my pj's tonight.

DAY 122: Blista Sista

So I have a couple of wicked blisters on my feet (first ones since I started training), and I've been a little under the weather this week and way overscheduled at work. I'm taking it a little easy this week but going to do my weekend walks in blocks of five this weekend. I have two blocks of five miles on Saturday and three blocks of five miles on Sunday. I have to do it like this because I am traveling.

I'm going on vacation next week, so I plan to do most of my walking outdoors to really build up my stamina.

I am sending love to my pal Sam, who is riding five hundred miles to raise money for cancer research. Rock on, cancer warrior!

She Defies Gravity

SAMANTHA

Sam is a girl with a dragon tattoo. Really. She has a dragon tattoo on her head. When she lost her hair during chemotherapy, in an attempt to stop the sympathetic stares directed toward her, she tattooed a dragon on her head. That way, the baldness became a sign that she was a badass, not that she was in a fight for her life.

Sam doesn't have breast cancer. She has ovarian cancer. She was thirty years old when she was diagnosed for the first time. Her doctor told her it was impossible for a thirty-year-old to have cancer. He doctor was wrong. Sam had stage II cancer.

As you know, this book and my story are about fighting breast cancer, but really, my mission is to uplift every woman who defies gravity. Sam has now beat ovarian cancer twice! After her initial diagnosis, she was cancer-free for almost three years. When she started to have pelvic pain, she was again told to wait and see, and once again, she pushed for tests and found out the cancer had returned. She went through yet another round of surgery and chemo.

Sam is a fierce warrior. She is an advocate in the fight against cancer and openly tells her story. On the day of The Walk, the city was cold and rainy, but Sam and her wonderful husband Mark came out in the dreary weather ringing a cowbell to support Team Defy Gravity. Sam's passion and energy are contagious. I am so lucky to know her and to bear witness to her remarkable journey.

Sam is now cancer free, and that damn dragon is still underneath her cute hair, which grows a bit longer every day.

CHAPTER 7

FINDING GRACE

*Living my best life is a tribute to the women who don't
have a choice, including my mother, who died at fifty-eight.
My mother and my sister did not live to see their sixtieth
birthdays. I'm going to be the woman in my family
who's ninety, dancing, and howling at the moon.*

—Grace

DAY 127: Stick Me with a Pin

Remember that vacation I mentioned? Well, I'm off on an adventure. I am spending a few days doing a medical immersion program. It's an opportunity to take a holistic look at my health—mind, body, and spirit. I am looking for ways to reduce stress in my life and to improve my own self-care.

Today, I was exposed to a couple of alternative treatments like acupuncture, which I have never tried before. It was an interesting experience. It was certainly a little odd to look down and see pins sticking out of my hands and feet. It didn't hurt, but I can't say I felt anything from the treatment. I also had a Reiki session, which was actually pretty relaxing. I have a yoga session tomorrow.

It has been one full week since I have walked or worked out. I was using my blisters as an excuse. So, tomorrow morning, I will head to the hotel gym and do three miles before I head back to my program.

DAY 128: Dogs, Cats, and Trees

I took my first private yoga class today, and it was actually kind of fun. I did something named after a dog, a cat, and a tree, and we weren't camping. The teacher adapted some of the moves specifically for me because lying on the floor on my back was really uncomfortable. She was very nice and really focused on what worked for me. One of the things that have kept me from being physically active (besides sheer laziness) has been feeling like I am so unfit I won't be able to keep up with the fit people in classes, so having this one-on-one instruction was really awesome. My fear was so much worse than the reality.

I walked three miles this morning and did the "hill" program on the treadmill, so I'm feeling good. I promise to do at least three or four miles in the morning before my last day of the program.

DAY 129: Now I Know What I Didn't Know

I didn't know that I would be able to keep up with the fitness trainer today and complete a full-circuit workout, keeping pace with my class.

I didn't know that I would be thrilled to see a twenty-year-old sweating just as much as I was.

I didn't know that 99 percent of the food I am eating is making my body do some things that are more significant than just being heavy.

I didn't know I was so tired that I just needed a break. I didn't know blueberries were so good for you. I didn't know how much I just needed to stop.

There's just lots I didn't know.

DAY 131: The Women I Love

This week, I was asked about the kinds of relationships I have in my life. I was asked if I feel as if I have a strong community and network of people who care about me. I am so blessed to be able to say yes. I have many dear male friends, but today I am grateful for the wonderful women in my life. They are smart, funny, kind, sassy, brave, scared, passionate, strong, courageous, willing, spunky, creative, and just plain freakin' fantastic.

Some of my friends are in difficult places in their lives. Some are moms. Some have never been married. Some are without children. Each of these wonder women is a light in my life. I am blessed beyond belief. I am in love with these women.

AY 133: Chip, Chip, Chip ... and Not the Kind in Cookies

I have packed a bag full of healthy snacks for the office because I tend to eat when I'm busy and stressed. Just adding more fruits and veggies into my diet as well. So, all in all, I am chipping away at my health, food, and training issues. Chip, chip, chip.

Day 136: Fall Risk

So, today was colonoscopy and endoscopy day. Woohoo! Double the pleasure, double the fun. Anyway, I got both tests out of the way, but honestly, the worst part is the liquid you have to drink to prep for the colonoscopy. The procedures don't hurt at all (of course, I was completely knocked out), but they put this huge, bright yellow band around my wrist before the drugs that said, "Fall Risk." They do this because it's common for the drugs to make you loopy.

When it was over, the nurse called four of us at the same time in the waiting room, all women. She asked each of us our names and who was going to escort us home. The answers were:

"I'm _____, and my husband is here in the waiting room."

"I'm _____, and my husband is waiting for me in the waiting room."

"I'm _____, and my husband is waiting for me in the waiting room."

"I'm Grace, and is it wrong to say I'm doing the happy dance my husband isn't my husband anymore? My pal Deb is picking me up."

So, you can only imagine how excited my pal Deb was as the person who had to get me home after the procedure. I am sure she prayed like a fiend that my big butt wouldn't be rolling down the street in Philly with her having to pick me up! She was a sweetheart to come get me.

Fall risk, my eye—I'm standing on my own!

DAY 138: What Would I Do for Me?

The doctor told me I am sleep-deprived just based on the number of hours I sleep per night (which is five, in case you were wondering), and I don't nap. I have been telling my pals that I have been gaining weight, and they all keep saying, "You don't look it," or "It's muscle from walking." Well, I am officially thirty pounds heavier than I was last year. I am officially at a number that I haven't seen in a very long time, and that scares the bajeezus out of me. This is craziness. I am tired and stressed out, and I overeat to keep myself moving. I was so disappointed and disheartened when I saw and heard that number. I wanted to cry, and I think I did inside.

I don't know why this has been my dragon all these years. I just know that I packed my walking shoes and am going to walk six miles tonight before I go home. I just want to cry. I'm going to say it. I feel fat and unattractive. I feel tired. I feel overwhelmed by all of this. I don't care how pulled together my outside looks; my insides are pretty beat up today.

CHAPTER 8

DEFY GRAVITY

I think gravity is anything invisible that holds you down.
For me, gravity was weight, shame, and fear.

—Grace

DAY 139: Raindrops Keep Falling on My Head

Big hugs to Deb and Jodi. We walked between nine and ten miles last night. It's tough to walk that long after working all day. It was raining when we started, and it would have been really easy to just go to dinner or happy hour, but we pushed through it. We started underground in Center City, then headed outside. We walked all the way to Manayunk and had dinner. I would not have done it if I had been by myself. I made it home at 11:00 PM and got up to walk this morning with Sherita, but it was pouring. My goal is to do six to eight miles today. Deb and Jodi have been such troopers. They are really doing all of this to support me. I know that and can't express what it means to me. I love them both very much.

DAY 147: Bit of a Slump

So, I haven't walked since last Sunday because (1) I had a medical procedure, (2) it was a busy week, (3) I had a bad attitude, and (4) I was completely overtired. Wah! Wah! Wah! Woe is me. So, tomorrow night, I'm doing a walk. I have to: no excuses! I love supporting this walk, but I admit I am feeling overwhelmed by the training right now and just wish I were celebrating the end! Whine, whine, whine. So, this is the ungraceful, whiney, petty, and small part of me. Not pretty, but it's true.

DAY 151: Gotta Get Walking

I have really let my training slide off. I am swamped at work and leave the office so tired that I'm not getting my miles in. I am not traveling over the long weekend, so I will have to kick my walking into gear. The weather is spectacular right now, so I don't have any excuses.

DAY 153: Go Team Defy Gravity!

I'm so happy to say that my big, tall, handsome pal John offered to do my training walk with me today, and we logged 10.5 miles. Along the way, we bumped into a group of folks training for The Walk. It was pretty cool to see them. I started chatting with a guy from a team called Linda's Ladies. He was very, very nice, and when I told him my team was Team Defy Gravity, he knew who we were. And then when I told him my first name was Grace, he knew me! He had been reading my blog. How cool is that? I was so flattered. But the walk today still kicked my butt. I'll be walking tomorrow.

DAY 155: Seattle

I'm tired. I flew to Seattle today and have been going all day. I'm fighting the three-hour time change, but I did get down and walked two quick miles on the treadmill. I'm going to do five to six miles tomorrow. I'm working off fumes, but I'm not giving up!

DAY 161: Five More Weeks

Wow! It's hard to believe The Walk is only five weeks away. The training for this walk is hard! But I keep remembering why I am doing this. Breast cancer sucks. Jodi and I are doing 10.5 miles tomorrow morning. We are all freaking out about doing 60, but I keep telling myself that the wind will be at my back, and I only have to take one step at a time.

DAY 170: How Much Does a Spirit Weigh?

The walk is one month away. I am excited and terrified at the same time. I did six miles this morning at the gym and now am in the office for a few hours. I will do six to ten miles tomorrow, and my goal is to do a minimum of six miles every day this week. I am so amazed at my wonderful team. They are all working so hard to cross the finish line.

And it's official: I have not lost a single pound, but I have gained some things along the way that are very precious. I'm still a fat girl walking, but somehow, the size of my stomach and thighs feels a lot less important than the size of my spirit.

DAY 177: Blisters and Blessings

Sherita and I just walked ten miles. I am so glad she is back in town, and it was wonderful to walk and talk and get caught up. All of my Defy Gravity teammates that I've been speaking with are freaking out that the walk is only two weekends away. We are all still hoping to find that pair of magic socks and those perfect clothes to make the day go easier and faster. Regardless of how daunting this walk feels right now, even with all the blisters and long training walks, I am reminded of how blessed I am to be making this journey with friends like Sherita.

DAY 180: TDG Kicks into Gear

Suddenly, we are gear-crazed women. My teammates are reading all of the packing guides, and the flurry of activity has begun. We need sleeping bags, flashlights, tape, etc. We are packing fools. I just keep telling myself to breathe deep and take this one day at a time. I almost hyperventilated walking down the sleeping bag aisle at Target.

But I am so proud of my teammates. Many of them signed up to support me, and now they are knee-deep in this adventure, too. By the way, I did three miles on the treadmill this morning, and I'll be doing another three tomorrow to help keep myself limber.

DAY 188: The Little Engine that Could

How do I express my gratitude to the women on my team? We are truly the Little Engine that Could. First, I give them credit because they signed up; some have walked before, but some were as out of shape as me. I cajoled a couple (Yes, Deb and Jodi, that's you!), and although I got some teasing from them along the way, they are doing it!

We are women in our thirties, forties, fifties, and sixties. We are tall, thin, short, and fat. We are moms and not moms, and we come in every color of the rainbow. We don't all love the same, pray the same, or live the same, yet here we are. We are bold, brave, sassy, unexpected, and courageous survivors, leaders, friends, and sisters.

And then we have our nonwalking teammates who have helped raise money and our spirits. All of these women have been the wind at my back when I needed a push up the hill. What we have in common cannot be defined by any one thing except that we all have heart. There are women on this team that I have never seen, yet I already know them. Team Defy Gravity, I love you and thank you for all your passion and sass along the way.

Race Day! An Unfortunate Update

As some of you have heard, the Philadelphia area is experiencing very unseasonably cold and wet weather. The highs are in the low forties today and tomorrow, and rain is expected the entire time. As a result, the organizers of The Walk made a very difficult decision late yesterday and canceled the first two days of The Walk. After consulting with experts and taking stock of their resources, they simply couldn't justify sending thousands of people into harm's way. Concerns ranged from having enough medical staff to handle the cases of hypothermia that they feared would occur to the danger of drivers along the route having poor visibility.

At this point, they are still planning to conduct The Walk on Sunday. If they do, I'll be there with bells on, leading Team

Defy Gravity to honor as much of my commitment as I possibly can. I'm sad that I'm missing out on the experience of being in camp and meeting the many survivors and others that are a part of this event. I'm disappointed that I won't be able to reach my personal goal of completing the sixty miles, something that I was really hoping to do after all of the training I've done. However, I know that the most important part of this has already been done!

I hope you will allow the hundreds of miles walked in training for this event to count towards our intentions. So, say a little prayer for better weather on Sunday, when we hope to walk fifteen miles to symbolize our commitment to the cure for breast cancer and keeping our promise to you.

CHAPTER 9

TURNING LEMONS INTO PINK LEMONADE

*I just have to keep on moving ... I am a force
of nature in process: stopping is not an option.*

—Grace

Yesterday Team Defy Gravity finished our journey at the closing ceremony of The Walk. Although the weather in Philadelphia made the event organizers cancel the first two days of the event, in the true spirit of defying gravity, many of us were out in the wet and cold Philly weather yesterday to finish what we started. We walked seventeen miles to honor our commitment to you and this cause.

We decided to make "pink lemonade" out of the "lemons" Mother Nature handed us. We suited up in ponchos, raingear, wool socks, and what I swear looks like the stuff you cover up your patio furniture with and headed out as the sun started to rise. We wore pink, blue, and bright neon-orange. We carried backpacks full of Band-Aids, moleskin, and dry socks. I also carried the unbelievable kindness and generosity of all of you with me.

You sent your money in just because I asked. You sent money because someone you love has or has had breast cancer. You sent your money because you know that any disease that affects one out of eight women must be cured. You sent money to honor your mothers, sisters, coworkers, bosses, wives, partners, and friends. You sent in money to honor Mary White.

But you did more than send money. You sent me notes, letters, flowers, care packages and everything pink under the sun. You went on training walks with me when I really didn't want to walk. You read my blog and worried about me when I said I was tired or sick. You encouraged me because you remembered that just a few years ago, I couldn't even walk four blocks because I was so out of shape and unhealthy. You reminded me that muscle weighs more than fat and helped me appreciate my body's significant physical transformation. You showed up on street corners with cowbells and signs to cheer us on. You showed up at the finish line and stood in the cold with cupcakes and champagne. You prayed.

So, thanks to all of your exceptional generosity, Team Defy Gravity raised nearly **one hundred thousand dollars** in the fight against breast cancer, and I have the honor of being the number one fundraiser in the city of Philadelphia, raising close to forty-five thousand dollars! I was able to lead the walkers in the closing ceremony with two fantastic women in my life who are breast cancer survivors, Elaine Yarbrough and Suzy Persutti. To be arm in arm with women who have fought this dragon and won made me forget that it was cold and wet outside. For those of you who have lost someone to this dreaded disease, they were with us yesterday, as well.

I am overwhelmed by your support, love, and kindness, and I hope you will allow me to raise some of that pink lemonade in *your* honor. Thank you, and please do something today to defy gravity!

CHAPTER 10

GRACE'S TOP TEN TIPS TO DEFY GRAVITY

1. **Find something you are passionate about and *do* something**. Writing a check is not enough. It helps, but it's only one channel. Be an advocate, an ambassador, or even an agitator. Passion is the difference between having a life and really living. Fighting for women with breast cancer and the eradication of this disease is something that stirs my passion.

2. **Kick whatever you fear in the butt**. Daylight is burning. Be afraid. Be angry. Be unsure. Then, get moving. Kick cancer in the butt for all the women who can't do it on their own.

3. **Declare yourself and your intentions.** Say it out loud. Fear and doubt usually live in the dark corners of our minds. Look your fear right in the eye and point a big ol' flashlight at it. I declared I would walk, and I did it. Now, I'm declaring I'm going to run ten miles in the spring of 2011. I'm scared out of my mind, but once I declare it, I create action to achieve it. Just to be clear, sometimes the first time I declare something it comes out sounding like a squeak. Eventually, the squeak becomes a roar. When you speak your intentions aloud, you tell your negative internal voice to shut the hell up.

4. **Name the boogieman**. I have women in my life that won't get mammograms or gynecological exams because

they think that if they don't "know" there is something wrong with them, then the problem doesn't exist. The boogieman exists even when it doesn't have a name. When you name it, then you can deal with it. Knowledge is power. Not knowing is telling ourselves we can't handle something. Defying gravity is only possible when you know what it is you need to defy.

5. **Know the difference between a network and a support group.** If there is wine and crying, it's a support group. If there is an exchange of power, information, and opportunity, then it's a network. Have both. Use them both. You don't have to like everyone in your network. Get over it. Sometimes, the woman or person you are the least attracted to has information that might save your life.

6. **Love.** I mean it. Love your friends with all your heart. Have a love affair with your women friends. Delight in them. Laugh with them. Eat chocolate with them. Tell your story, and know their story. Laugh until you swear you are going to pee your pants. Plan trips. Have women in your life that are older but are willing to say, "To hell with being wise," and just opt for wonderful. Embrace younger women and learn from them. Being hip is important! If you don't have sisters, make sure you choose some to walk alongside you. When you are lying on the cold, tile floor in the bathroom and swear you can't get up because you are too physically sick, heartsick, or alone, these are the women who will pick you up and love you until you can love yourself.

7. **Be grateful and generous.** Gratitude without generosity is one-dimensional. Don't hoard your good fortune. Gratitude expressed through prayer is great. Gratitude expressed through generosity of time, money, energy, and kindness is what lifts us beyond ourselves

and moves us into our full power. Share what you know; extend a kindness to a stranger. Be especially kind to women. Sometimes, the compliment you pay to a stranger or the door you hold for a woman struggling with a stroller or packages is the only kindness that woman will experience that day, that month, or that year. Play nice. Please count your blessings more than you count your calories.

8. **Don't live your life looking in the rearview mirror.** Look ahead. Drive forward. It's okay if you can't see the destination, but looking back all the time only guarantees you will miss what is coming toward you. When you drive at night, you can only see as far as your headlights. You trust that there is more road in front of you. Live your life the same way. You can look back, but please don't stare.

9. **Be willing to ask for and to accept help**. Sometimes, the only way out of the darkness is to let someone hold the flashlight for you. Grab her hand. Cry on her shoulder. You don't ever have to be alone. Needing help is not about weakness. It takes courage to admit we are lonely and afraid. Nobody ever said you had to defy gravity alone.

10. **Celebrate.** Do your own version of the happy dance. Recognize how far you have come even if it's only one inch further than you went the day before. It's an inch! Defying gravity is a journey, not a destination. Give yourself an atta girl now and again. Get that pedicure, or meet that friend for lunch. Do what makes you feel like the fantastic, amazing, unique, and powerful woman that you are!

2010 Final Flash

November 23, 2010

Dear friends, coworkers, Betsy's and champions,

I am on the plane home to Philadelphia after completing the three-day Walk in San Diego. Your generous support helped Team Defy Gravity raise over sixty thousand dollars for the cure! In total, the San Diego walk raised ten million dollars this weekend!

Many of you know I started this journey last year as a call to action when Mary White died. My own physical health was at risk due to my lifelong struggle with obesity. At nearly 350 pounds, I couldn't walk four blocks without taking a cab.

Yesterday, I completed a sixty-mile journey to reclaim my own health and to support the women in our lives who are too often touched by this terrible disease. I am thrilled to tell you that I walked every single mile of the sixty miles. Strong. Fit. Powerful. Since 2007, I have lost over 120 pounds; however, it's not what I've lost that matters—it's what I've found.

I found that moving from pissed off to passionate can really create change. I found my inner athlete. I found gratitude at a deep and profound level for all of my blessings. I found people like you who have cheered me on in every way imaginable.

I found out that Vaseline and good socks can keep you blister free. I found teammates who are incredible women that didn't let a little thing like sixty miles keep them from showing up!

I found inspiration in the men and women who stood along the road and cheered us on in terrible weather. I found many people who do the work of angels.

I found old friends and new ones visiting my hometown of San Diego. I found my mother's spirit, as Thea's daughter climbed the hills her mother traveled as a little girl.

I found myself praying for all of the women and men in my life and yours who have so bravely fought and are fighting breast cancer today. I found myself laughing when I was so wet and cold that there just wasn't anything to do but laugh. I found deep gratitude when I turned the corner and saw a women dressed in green and holding a sign that said "Defy Gravity" while the song that inspired me so much was playing on her car stereo.

I found awe when a double rainbow peeked out of the grey San Diego sky as we literally crossed the finish line on day two. On a day where the winds whipped the rain at us for hour upon hour, the rainbow was an amazing sight.

Now, it's time to finally find a cure!

Thank you from the bottom of my heart for helping me to defy gravity.

LaVergne, TN USA
20 January 2011
213170LV00002B/2/P